MY PERSONAL WEIGHT LOSS CHALLENGE

How I Lost 52 lbs. in Five Months

By

F.V. Flores

DISCLAIMER

Before starting this or any other diet, consult your physician of the Weight Loss Challenge you are interested in embarking on. Please do as your physician suggests. Embarking on this Weight Loss Challenge will be your decision and at your own risk. When purchasing this booklet, you are agreeing to this disclaimer and the author will not assume responsibility of any results.

TABLE OF CONTENTS

1. *BEFORE STARTING THIS WEIGHT LOSS CHALLENGE*

This personal weight loss challenge is a combination of motivation and dedication which includes vitamins and a limited food source for the first (few) week(s).

Before starting this weight loss challenge, I must advise, this is what worked for me. I do not guarantee that by following this extreme diet plan, you will achieve your desired weight loss goals.

Taking the vitamins I used in this diet is an optional decision and at your own discretion. The vitamins listed are only listed to indicate the type of vitamins I used during my commitment to this weight loss challenge. It does not necessarily mean that by taking these specific vitamins, your personal weight loss goals will be achieved.

2. *INTRODUCTION*

No one ever believes how easy it is to lose weight when you really set your mind to it and are willing to do all you have to in order to achieve your desired weight goals. For years, I have been trying one diet after another and my weight has gone up and down. I was never able to reach my ideal weight loss goals. I would give up and try again numerous times.

Finally, one day, I said to myself, "That's it! Enough! I will lose the weight I want and I will keep it off." There was no changing my mind. I figured I have already tried everything I could think of to lose weight, so why not this?

My boyfriend is into sports and completely dedicated to physical health and fitness. One day, I told him of my plans with this challenge and I asked him for advice in the type of exercise I should do to help me achieve my weight loss goals and, at the same time, help keep my body well-toned. His suggestions were very helpful to me. We started going to the gym more often. At the gym, he taught me sets of different types of exercises to do so I can stay fit and my body toned. Now, a year later, I have made exercising a part of my lifestyle. I now go to the gym almost every day. And of course, I am very happy with the results.

Right before Thanksgiving 2016, my goals were set and The Weight Loss Challenge began. As most of us already know, the Thanksgiving holiday is one of the times of the year where people over indulge in food they do not partake in most of the year. Throughout the holidays, I believe, the average person will eat as much as possible and wait to lose the weight they gain after the holidays; usually as a New Year's Resolution that may or may not work.

By starting this dietary challenge during the holidays, it was a way to prove to myself just how much self-control I can have.

When I started this challenge, November 23rd, 2016, I weighed exactly 192lbs. I have not weighed this much since giving birth to my youngest child who is now 10 years old. For Thanksgiving dinner, November 24, 2016, I wore a size 12 dress. Five months later, April 2017, I was weighing exactly 145lbs and wearing a size 6 in clothing. Five months…. Who can believe that? No one can. The pictures in pages below illustrated my Before and After pictures. Wait until you see the difference.

It is now December 2017, and I am now wearing a size 4 in clothing and weighing 140lbs. I have not been dieting for months. Now I can eat everything and anything I want. I am happy to say I am now the weight and clothes size I've been wanting to be for years.

I believe the reason my weight and clothes size have remained the same throughout the year even though I eat everything I want, is because I was committed to my goal and determined to reach my ideal weight. I am no longer trying to lose weight. Below, I explain in more detail why eating everything I want still has me at my ideal weight.

3. *LET'S START THAT PERSONAL WEIGHT LOSS CHALLENGE*

Again, I must advise, before starting this or any other diet, consult your physician. If not recommended by your physician, do not take part in this challenge. And as stated earlier in the booklet, taking the vitamins used during this dietary challenge is an optional decision and at your own discretion. The vitamins listed were only the ones I used to achieve my personal weight loss goals. It is not guaranteed that by using these different vitamins, your personal weigh loss goals will also be achieved.

When beginning this challenge, I bought a Poster Size Chart and in big bolded letters, I wrote down my ideal weight goals. My ideal weight goal was to weigh between 135-140lbs. Under that weight loss goal, I taped a picture of myself weighing 192lbs. Next to that picture, I left a blank space to eventually tape a picture of the results, which I have already done.

Don't get me wrong, this challenge is not an easy task to follow. At the beginning, it is very hard to stay on track and resist, but willpower and motivation will do the job. The few times I felt a bit overwhelmed and had particular food temptations or when I thought of giving up, I redirected my thoughts and went right to where I had the chart with my weight loss goals and that picture of myself. Seeing that picture was motivation enough not to cheat on my diet. When I did feel tempted and wanted to eat something that might interfere with this challenge, I would go out for a walk, back to the gym, or did just about anything that would get my mind away from food.

Of course, after I was set and steady working my weight down to the level I wanted, I did not deny myself a treat once in a while. Not over doing it in quantity, with whatever treat, I would have with my weight loss goal in mind and lots of water to follow. I accomplished what I wanted. As stated earlier, now I can eat anything and it doesn't affect me in anyway. I take a couple of bites of my meal and I am already full. I can honestly say, I have not finished a meal in months.

Below is a list of instructions or ideas to go by when attempting this weight loss challenge. The list below is recommended to be followed even after the first week's challenge is complete. By following this list, I have been able to continue living a healthy and active lifestyle at the weight I originally set my goals to. Now, over a year since starting this weight loss challenge, my stomach has shrunk. A shrunken stomach is not necessarily bad. By stating a shrunken stomach, I mean I can now eat all I want and will get full extremely fast.

Once you are an adult, your stomach pretty much remains the same size – unless you have surgery to intentionally make it smaller. Eating less won't shrink your stomach, says Moyad, but it can help to reset your "appetite thermostat" so you won't feel as hungry, and it may be easier to stick with your eating plan. Jun 6, 2013.

I can't remember the last time I went out with my boyfriend and I finished an entire meal. I have honestly thought of at times ordering a "Kid's Meal" instead.

www.webmd.com/women/features/stomach-problems

4. REASONS FOR WEIGHT LOSS

1. *According to the Center for Disease Control (CDC), in 2011-2014, the prevalence of obesity was just over 36% in adults and 17% in youth. The prevalence of obesity was higher in women (38.3%) than in men (34.3%). Among youth, there was no difference in sex.*

2. *Obesity and inactivity have cost American tax payers billions of dollars. In 2008, the estimated annual medical cost of obesity was $147 billion.*

3. *"On average, overweight people lose about one year of life expectancy, and moderately obese people lose about three years of life expectancy," said Dr. Emanuele Di Angelantonio, the lead author, from the University of Cambridge.*

4. *Weighing too much is really making people sick, and as per the CDC, obesity contributes to heart*

disease, strokes, type 2 diabetes, certain types of cancer, and some leading to preventable death.

5. As per personal experience, I know it can also become expensive when continuously having to purchase clothing to fit adequately.

6. With such a weight loss epidemic going on today, it can also become more and more expensive to regularly try out the different types of diets available.

7. You need to be realistic. For example, if you want to lose weight right now, at this very moment, realize that that is not possible and it is not a reasonable goal to set because it will not happen. You need to be patient and completely dedicated, and finally work hard to achieve the weight loss goals you want to accomplish.

8. Learn about and understand how to Portion the size of the food you consume. You can

practically eat anything you want as long as you portion your food size correctly.

9. *Think of this as "The less you eat, the smaller you will become." That's how I thought of my food portions and now I am the size I want to be and I am determined to stay at this weight. The good thing about this challenge, is that it is not really as expensive as other diets and I can go back and started when I feel I need to. Believe it or not, I gave away over 150lbs of clothing I wore, sizes 10 and 12 within the five months after I completed my challenge.*

www.cdc.gov/obesity/data/adult.html
www.theguardian.com>society>obesity

5. *INSTRUCTIONS WHEN ATTEMPTING THE WEIGHT LOSS CHALLENGE*

ALWAYS REMEMBER THE FOLLOWING:

1. ***EXERCISE, EXERCISE, EXERCISE:***

   Exercise daily for 90 minutes. The 90 minutes can be divided into minutes or done all at once; 90 minutes straight, 30-30-30, or 45-45. (Do not do less, do not do more than the 90 minutes in order to avoid over exhaustion).

2. *Every time water is indicated in this booklet, it refers to 8-16oz of water. If you decide to drink more water than indicated, water is good.*

3. *Bananas are not allowed with this diet and completely forbidden during first seven days because of its high sugar content.*

4. *Sodas and any other type of soft drink is not allowed at all. It is recommended to discard soft*

drinks out of daily diet altogether, but to your discretion after the challenge.

5. *Small portions of food are recommended or serve your normal size plate but make it a habit never to eat a full meal, always leave food on the plate, no matter how good it tastes. Do not serve yourself more food with the intentions of not finishing the meal because that would be defeating the purpose and you will only be cheating yourself.*

6. *Always, and on a regular basis after the challenge, try to eat 5-6 times per day in small portions. The idea is to get your stomach to close-up naturally. After at least two months of following this strict diet, you will notice how fast you will get full.*

7. *Eat Food Loaded with Protein (the more protein the better).*

8. *Drink 2% or lower Milk (Or milk such as Soy Milk, or SILK Milk, etc.).*

9. *Walk as much as possible.*

10. *Don't sit around all day doing nothing or watching TV or in different forms of social media. Go window shopping, help clean the house, Vacuum, go up and down the stairs if bored, wash the car, go to the gym or a park, etc. (Be active. The idea is to make yourself sweat as much as possible).*

11. *When food shopping, if not for so much food that you would need a cart. carry a basket instead and it will be like lifting smaller weights.*

12. *Make sports a hobby; play tennis, go skating, play football, basketball, baseball, etc. Try to make exercising a lifestyle.*

13. *When at work, try to park the car as far as possible from your office or work area.*

14. *Remember to use you daily activities as a motivation to help you reach goals faster.*

6. *FOOD LIST AND SIZE*

1. **Coffee:** *(Any type of coffee, limit sugar to 1 teaspoon, substitute sugar not recommended but optional).*

2. **Crackers:** *(Saltine, Premium or any other similar Crackers). 1-size Crackers= 2 single crackers (i.e., when suggesting 3-4-size crackers, the plan is actually suggesting 6-8 single crackers).*

3. **Baked Fish:** *Preferably, fresh fish. If too much, save in the freezer for a later date. Season and bake in oven or toaster oven. It should only take a few minutes to cook since fish cooks really fast.*

4. **Boiled Chicken:** *Boil the chicken yourself so you can see exactly how much less fat you are eating. If you boiled too much chicken, save the rest in freezer and save for a later date. (Seasoning is optional).*

5. **Protein:** *Bars and/or Drinks. (Any brand is good, recommend ones higher in grams).*

6. **Small Fruits:** *Small apples, pears, 6-8 grapes, 3-4 strawberries, ¼ cup of berries, etc. Be conscious of small amounts of fruit. (Remember, no Bananas due to high in sugar).*

7. **Small Salads:** *Lettuce, Spinach, Romaine or Cabbage salads. Add small amounts of carrots, tomatoes, raisins, croutons, etc.*

8. **Tuna:** *Use Flavored Tuna, no name brand in particular. Do not use canned tuna. By using Flavored Tuna, you will not need to use Mayonnaise as it is already flavored. Flavored Tuna packs are easy to find in grocery stores.*

9. **Veggies:** *Small amounts of veggies such as mixed, peas, carrots, broccoli, etc.*

10. **Water:** *Water refers to 8-16oz of water. If more water is desired, optional.*

11. **Yogurt:** *For this part of the challenge, it will be your choice on brand of yogurt to eat. During my weight loss challenge, I used Activia. No matter the*

yogurt you eat, please do try to eat same yogurt brand daily.

7. DAILY VITAMINS

1. *Super B-Complex*

2. *B-12 1000mcg*

3. *Biotin   5000mcg*

4. *Black Seed Vegetarian Capsules (Either Liquid or Pills)*

5. *Ultimate 10 Probiotic*

6. *CoQ10 100mg*

7. *Mega Red Advance 4 in 1 Extra Strength 900mg*

8. *Collagen Advance Formula Type 1, 2, 3 with 18 Amino Acids*

9. *Calcium Citrate Magnesium and Zinc with VitaminD3*

10. *Carnipure l-Carnitine 500-1100mg (Either Liquid or pills)*

11. *Garcinia Cambodia*

8. *FIRST THREE DAYS: CHALLENGE*

LIST TO FOLLOW

TAKE DAILY VITAMINS BEFORE BREAKFAST

BREAKFAST: *Coffee with 3-4-Size Crackers*

SNACK: *Coffee or water with 2-4-size Crackers*

LUNCH: *Water, package of Flavored Tuna and 3-4-Size Crackers*

SNACK: *Water with 3-4-Size Crackers*

DINNER CHOICES: *(Alternate Meals during the three day challenge)* **(1)** *Tuna, Water, 3-4-Size Crackers and small fruit.* **(2)** *Boiled Chicken, water, 3-4-Size Crackers and small fruit.* **(3)** *Baked Fish, water, 3-4-Size Crackers and small fruit.* **(4)** *Small Salad, water, 3-4-Size Crackers and small fruit.*

SNACK: *Water and 3-4-Size Crackers*

BEDTIME: *Water*

9. *SECOND THREE DAYS: CHALLENGE*

LIST TO FOLLOW

TAKE DAILY VITAMINS BEFORE BREAKFAST

BREAKFAST: *Coffee with 3--Size Crackers*

SNACK: *Water and Protein Bar or Protein Drink*

LUNCH: *Small salad, water, and small fruit (No Bananas) or 6-8 grapes or 3-4 strawberries.*

SNACK: *Water with 3-4-Size Crackers or water with opposite Protein of morning snack.*

DINNER CHOICES: (1) *Small salad, water, 3-4-Size Crackers and small side of veggies.* **(2)** *Flavored Tuna pkg., water, 3-4-Size Crackers and small side of veggies.* **(3)** *Boiled Chicken, water, 3-4-Size Crackers and small side of veggies.* **(4)** *Baked Fish, water, 3-4-Size Crackers and small side of veggies.*

SNACK: *Water and 3-4-Size Crackers*

BEDTIME: *Water*

10. *SEVENTH DAY: LAST CHALLENGE*

LIST TO FOLLOW

ALWAYS REMEMBER TO TAKE AM VITAMINS BEFORE BREAKFAST

BREAKFAST: *Coffee with 3-4-Size Crackers*

SNACK: *Water with Protein Bar or Protein Drink*

LUNCH: *Salad with meat in it (Chicken, Steak, Pork, or Tuna), small fruit or Yogurt or small size vegies.*

SNACK: *Opposite of Morning snack*

DINNER: *Lite Dinner but don't over-do it. Limit Portion and remember your earlier efforts for the target goals.*

SNACK: *Water and 3-4-Size Crackers*

BEDTIME: *Water*

11. *SUGGESTED EXERCISES TO HELP KEEP YOUR BODY TONED*

1. *10-15lbs Weight Lifting Exercises*

2. *6 Minutes ABS Exercises*

3. *30 Crunches*

4. *10 Minutes Walking*

5. *6 Minutes Running or Climbing*

6. *15 Minutes Dancing*

7. *20 Minutes Swimming*

8. *6 Minutes Pilates*

9. *30 Planks*

10. *8-10 Push-Ups/Pull-Ups*

11. *10-15 Hip Raise/Butt Lift Bridge*

12. *45 seconds Sit with a Twist*

13. *10 Leg Pull-In/Knee-Up*

14. *10-15 Plank Jacks/Extended Knees*

15. *10-15 Lying Leg Raise/Lift*

16. *15-20 Squats*

17. .   *45 Seconds Wall Sits*

18.   *15-20 Jumping Jacks*

19.   *15 Lunges each side*

****Repeat Diet as Needed and Enjoy a Healthy and Active Lifestyle****
Good Luck
F.V. Flores, MBA, MSW

12.   *BEFORE AND AFTER PICTURES*

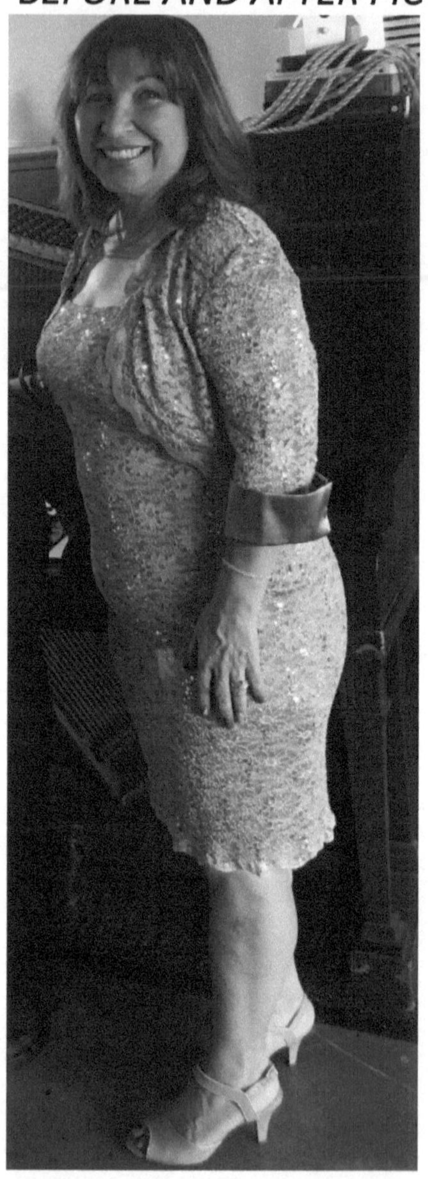

November 2016

November 2017